Literacy Activities for Early Childhood Classrooms

for

Morrow

Literacy Development in the Early Years
Helping Children Read and Write

Fourth Edition

prepared by

Lesley Mandel Morrow
The State University of New Jersey

Elizabeth Brown Asbury
The State University of New Jersey

Allyn and Bacon
Boston London Toronto Sydney Tokyo Singapore

ISBN 0-205-33630-2

Printed in the United States of America

10 9 8 7 6 5 4 3   05 04 03 02 01

This supplement provides lesson plans that coincide with each of the ten chapters in the book *Literacy Development in the Early Years: Helping Children Learn to Read and Write*. The plans were written by classroom teachers and provide a model for current exemplary practice in early literacy.

Chapter 1 lays the theoretical foundation for early literacy education. The lesson plans for this chapter are:

📖 Court is Now in Order

📖 I Can Read on my Own

These lessons put the theories of Montessori and of whole language into practice.

Chapter 2 deals with assessment and meeting the diverse individual needs of students. The plans for this chapter are:

📖 You Write, I Write

📖 Today I Learned . . .

These lessons demonstrate the use of authentic assessment.

Chapter 3 focuses on creating strong family literacy partnerships. There are three lesson plans in this section as follows:

📖 Reading Parents

📖 Thematic Backpacks

📖 A Pajama Party

These lessons provide ideas for interactive activities that promote family involvement in children's literacy development.

Chapter 4 covers the topic of oral language. The plans include:

📖 Monthly Poetry Recital

📖 What Am I Wearing?

These plans provide motivational contexts for oral language development and second language learners.

Chapter 5 addresses the role of technology among other topics. The plans are:

📖 Exploring Word Processing

📖 Visit the White House on a Virtual Tour

Creative ways to help children become computer literate and familiar with the World Wide Web are described in these lessons.

Chapter 6 focuses upon issues of motivating reading and writing through the use of children's literature. The plans that complement this chapter are:

📖 A Story Retelling of *The Foot Book* by Dr. Seuss

📖 A Story Retelling of *The Hungry Caterpillar* by Eric Carle

📖 Letter Writing to Corduroy the Bear

Each plan suggests ways to effectively motivate active engagement and skill development through authentic literature.

Chapter 7 deals with comprehension. The plans for this chapter are:

📖 Character Connections

📖 An Introduction to Graphic Organizers

These plans offer activities that help children read with a purpose and read for meaning.

Chapter 8 addresses developing reading through word study strategies. The plans are:

📖 Integrating Phonics into the Morning Message

📖 Understanding Homophones

These plans describe ways to integrate phonics instruction into meaningful contexts.

Chapter 9 focuses upon writing development. The plans for this chapter include:

📖 Script a Play

📖 Journal Starters

Two motivational contexts for facilitating writing development are presented in these lessons.

Chapter 10 concentrates on issues related to organization and management. The plans for this chapter are:

📖 Finding a "Just Right" Book for Independent Reading

📖 A Small Group Guided Reading Lesson for Early Readers

In these plans, teachers are provided with a model for explicit instruction and a concrete method for teaching children how to self-select reading material.

Acknowledgements

We would like to express our thanks and appreciation to the following individuals: Elizabeth Brown for drawing the diagrams and proofreading, Jordan Ullman for editing and proofreading, and Christine Wojnicki for formatting and generating the graphics. Most of all we thank the teachers who have generously contributed their time and expertise in designing lessons that support children's literacy development in the early years.

Title: Court Is Now in Order

This lesson integrates social studies and literacy instruction. Integrated and theme-oriented instruction emerged during the whole language movement. This lesson may be carried out as a culminating activity for a thematic unit on Fairy Tales.

Objectives: Children will have the opportunity to:
1. Gain knowledge of the various roles played by those involved in the justice system.
2. Take part in constructing a court case based upon information gleaned through literal, inferential, and critical comprehension of a fairy tale.
3. Participate in a mock trial.

Materials: Copy of the story *Goldilocks and the Three Bears*, paper, pencils, and pens for student writing.

Activity:

📖 Familiarize the students with the fairy tale of *Goldilocks and the Three Bears*. Discuss the various perspectives of each character in the story and how the story could be changed depending upon which story character tells the story. Compare and contrast the story from Goldilocks' and the bears' points of view. This may be done over several days.

📖 Meanwhile, begin to introduce the students to the different responsibilities of those who work within the judicial system. Include the following: plaintiff, defendant, lawyer, sheriff's officer, court clerk, jury, and judge. You may want to bring in guest speakers from the community. Lawyers came to my class to explain what it is like to be in a courtroom.

📖 Have each child decide upon a role that they would like to play in the trial of Goldilocks vs. The Three Bears. The roles include the plaintiff (all three bears may participate in the trial), the defendant, at least two lawyers, the sheriff's officer, the court clerk (students may take turns), members of the jury, and the judge who may be played by the principal.

📖 Prepare for the trial by having the students work together to write the script for the trial. Students must develop questions for the lawyers to ask the witnesses. The witnesses must also be prepared with answers. Make a copy of the final script for each student.

📖 On the day of the trial, conduct the case using the prepared script. The jury may leave the room to deliberate the verdict and to determine a fair and reasonable punishment if applicable. (The verdict of our case was that Goldilocks was found guilty of vandalism and breaking and entering. Her punishment was to cook porridge for the Three Bears for a week and a $50.00 fine to replace the broken chair.)

Variations:

📖 Have the children prepare a mock trial for other stories, such as *The Three Little Pigs* or *Little Red Riding Hood*.

📖 Costumes can be created for the various roles the children assume.

📖 The children may enjoy hearing *The True Story of the Three Little Pigs* by Jon Scieszka.

Stefanie Zamlong, Second Grade Teacher

Title: I Can Read On My Own!:
An Independent Reading Activity

This activity takes place in a context where the children work independent of the teacher. Several aspects of Montessori's theory are embedded in this activity. First, the children are working at their own level and at their own pace. Individual needs are accommodated. Next, specific steps are taught to the children that facilitate their ability to work on their own. For example, the last step of the lesson provides students with a means for self-correction. Last, we see evidence of a prepared environment wherein the materials are organized and labeled for easy access.

Objectives: Children will have the opportunity to:

1. Engage in independent reading of books previously read in small guided reading groups.
2. Practice using picture clues and print as meaningful sources of information.
3. Further understand the concept of sequencing.

Materials: Copies of books read during small group instruction, two enrichment papers for each title per child, materials to complete enrichment papers: pencils, glue, scissors, file folders-one per text, materials to make a self-correction chart: samples of completed, enrichment pages; pieces of fabric approximately 9" by 12" –one per text.

Activity:

📖 Group the books in bins according to the leveling system used with the reading series. Some series may level books according to colors, others to letters or numbers. Depending upon the number of guided reading groups in your class, most bins will contain multiple copies of up to three titles.

📖 Explain to the children that they are to choose texts from a particular bin. They will know they have chosen the correct bin when they see the book they read in guided reading located in the bin.

📖 Prepare two enrichment activity pages to go along with each book. One sheet will simply have the book title and the author's name written in large font. The other sheet will also have the book title and the author's name as well as a single copy of sentences from the story in non-sequential order. Each sentence will be outlined in a solid, black box. Place the enrichment pages in a folder stapled on both sides so that it forms a pocket. Label the folder with the book title and author and place it in the bin along with the books.

📖 Instruct the children to select their text from the bin and find the folder with the matching title. They will also take one copy of each enrichment activity sheet.

📖 Model for the children how to cut the sentences apart. Then, using the book as a guide, they are to glue the sentences in sequential order onto the paper that bears the book title and author's name.

📖 After completing the activity, the children will check their work at the "Magic Curtains." (See diagram.) This may be located on a bulletin board or you may use a poster board. The "Magic Curtains" are pieces of cloth that resemble curtains. Behind each piece of fabric is a sample of the completed work in the correct sequential order. The children will be instructed how to locate their book title and will open the "Magic Curtains" in order to check their work.

📖 Checked papers are placed in a bin that is located alongside the "Magic Curtains" self-correcting board.

Variations:

📖 Enrichment sheet activities may vary according to the skill you wish to have the children develop. For example, you may have children write definitions to words that are found in the text using inference and context clues.

Joanne R. Coppola, Kindergarten Teacher

Chapter 2: Observing and Assessing the Needs of All Children

Title: You Write, I Write:
Using Interactive Writing as a Means of Authentic Assessment

Objectives: The children will have the opportunity to:
1. Write interactively with the teacher.
2. Work at their individual level of development while being supported to gain new understanding about how our language works.

Materials: Children's journals, markers and pencils for student's use, black felt tip pen for teacher's use.

Activity:

📖 During journal time, pull aside one student or a small group of students to conduct an interactive writing activity. Have the students bring their journals and materials for drawing and writing.

📖 Give the students two to three minutes to think of a topic about which they want to write. For some, they will start by drawing a picture. Others will begin writing.

📖 Interact with the children as they write. Ask them to tell you about what they are writing and prompt them at their point of need. For example, " What sound do you hear at the beginning of that word? What letter makes that sound? Can you hear any sounds at the end of the word? How about in the middle?" For more fluent writers, encourage them to elaborate upon their ideas. For example, "If you added some describing words I would be able to clearly see that picture in my mind."

📖 Encourage the child to do as much of the problem solving and writing as possible. They may refer to word walls, charts, and other print sources in the classroom. When the child needs more support, write that which the child could not write using the felt tip pen. For example, a child may be able to record beginning and ending sounds in words but is developing hearing middle sounds. A word in their journal may look like the following: h**ear**t (bold print is the teacher's writing). You may note other areas in the journal entry where strong teacher support was required by marking a dot at the beginning of the passage and a dot at the end, indicating where you helped the child.

📖 Make sure to use lots of specific, positive praise in your interactions. For example, "Placing the exclamation point at the end of that sentence was perfect. I could tell you really were surprised when you found what the tooth fairy left for you."

📖 By looking over the children's journals, you can see progress over time as well as the children's areas of need. You may, for example, see the need to teach certain sight words, punctuation usage, or prefixes and suffixes. These can be addressed in whole group shared reading and writing lessons or in a one-to-one context. As the year progresses it is rewarding to both the children and the teacher to see the student's participation in the interactive writing increase while the teacher's decreases.

Variations:

📖 You may use this interactive writing process for composing morning messages, stories, etc. with the class.

📖 Parent volunteer and cross-age peer tutors may be taught how to write interactively with the children.

Susan Yoder, Kindergarten Teacher

Title: Today I Learned…

Objectives: The children will have the opportunity to:
1. Reflect upon their learning on a daily basis.
2. Maintain an on-going record that chronicles knowledge they have constructed over time.
3. Participate in an activity that elicits thoughtful closure to the end of the school day.

Materials: Index cards- one per student per day, pens or pencils for student writing, hanging chart with one pocket for each student.

Activity:

📖 Hang the chart near the door of the classroom. Place a stack of index cards near the chart.

📖 Allow 10 minutes at the end of the day for children to complete this activity. As the children are gathering their things at the end of the day, direct them to pick up an index card and return to their seats prepared for dismissal.

📖 Take two to three minutes to briefly review the learning activities that took place that day making sure to highlight key concepts. Give the students two to three minutes to think about what was the most significant or meaningful concept, skill, etc. they learned that day. Instruct the students to write their thoughts about the day's learning onto their index card.

📖 Have the students "pair and share" with a partner. Each one will read what they wrote which will take about three minutes.

📖 As the children exit the classroom, they place their card into the appropriate pocket on the hanging chart. By reviewing these cards on occasion, you can gain insight into what concepts the children have understood and recalled correctly.

Variations:

📖 The cards may be sent home at the end of the week so that parents may be kept up to date about their child's learning. You may encourage parents to use the cards as a source of discussion with their child. Some will voluntarily extend what has been learned in school with at-home activities.

📖 You may prefer to have the children keep their cards in school and at the end of the school year, compile them into a book entitled, "I Learned A Lot This Year!" The students are amazed and very proud when they realize all they learned throughout the school year.

Christine Zehnder, Graduate School of Education Student

Title: Reading Parents

Objectives: The children will have the opportunity to:
1. Develop fluency in oral reading.
2. Increase confidence and comfort in reading by developing a one-on-one relationship with a parent volunteer.

Materials: A cozy corner for the parent volunteer and student to read together, books selected by the teacher or students for reading to the parent.

Activity:

📖 Introduce the idea of Reading Parents at Back-to-School Night. Determine which parents are interested in reading with children individually or in small groups throughout the school year. Make up a schedule of volunteers providing them with a day and time that they will come to read aloud or hear the children read to them. Group the children according to the parents' schedules' so they become Monday Readers, Tuesday Readers, etc.

📖 When the parent arrives s/he goes to the designated reading area. The first child who is prepared to read proceeds to the reading area. After reading with the parent for about 5 minutes, the child quietly lets the next child know it is their turn to read. When all the children have read, the parent can quietly leave with little or no interruption to the class routine.

📖 You may choose to assign a small book for reading, such as a vowel-intensive story or a theme-related book, before the children begin to make their own book choices. This allows the teacher to have the children work on a specific skill area in their reading.

📖 The parents do not have to keep any written record of the children's progress but often like to quietly comment to me about the great improvement they see in the children as the year progresses. Parents may be asked to keep a reading log for each child wherein they record the book title and author and can make additional comments about the session.

Suggestions for Success:
Meet with all the Reading Parents before the start of the program.
Discuss the following points:

📖 The need to remain positive toward the children at all times.

📖 Make them aware that the children assigned to them will be on different reading levels. It is imperative that they do not discuss any child's ability with another parent outside the school setting.

📖 Non-readers can be read to until they have made enough progress to do their own reading.

📖 Discuss effective ways to help children who "get stuck" on words and need assistance.

Joan M. Robinson, Kindergarten Teacher

Title: Thematic Backpacks

Objectives: The children will have the opportunity to:
1. Participate in shared reading and theme-related activities at home.
2. Nurture literacy development through parental engagement.

Materials: Backpack, 5-7 books that represent a variety of genre and reading levels, a folder with games, poems, songs, and/or experiments related to the theme under study, other related items such as videos, cassette tapes, stuffed animals, etc., class journal.

Activity:

📖 Assemble the theme-based backpack including directions and all necessary materials.

📖 The children take the backpack home weekly on a rotating basis. Instruct the children to share the activities and books with their family members. It may be helpful to show a backpack and model some of the activities for the parents at Back-to-School Night. They may also be put on display at Parent-Teacher Conferences so parents may become acquainted with the materials and procedures.

📖 Under parental guidance, the children respond to what is asked of them in the class journal that is in the backpack. The questions may include, "Which was your favorite book and why was it your favorite? " Or, to go along with a food theme for example, the children may be asked to share a family recipe. A music theme may include a tape recorder and blank tape to record a favorite song.

📖 When the backpack is returned to school, the child shares the journal response with the class. The kids and parents can hardly wait until it is their turn for the next backpack!

Variations:

📖 Mystery Box: Send an empty lunch box home weekly with one child. It is their job to work with a family member to find something to put into it to bring back to class. They must write three clues to help their classmates guess the secret item. On Friday, the clues are read and guesses are made. The Mystery Box is then sent home with another student.

📖 Items included in the Mystery Box may be related to a theme. Send home a note with the lunch box so that parents know what theme is currently under study.

Shannon Corcoran , Graduate School of Education Student

A Pajama Party!:
A Great Event to Spark School, Family, & Community Literacy Partnerships

The 'Pajama Party" is an event in which the children and teachers who choose to participate come to school for the evening dressed for bed, carrying a blanket, a favorite stuffed animal, and a favorite book. We hold this once-a-year event for kindergarten and first grade students and their parents and have a standing-room-only crowd in the school library.

The children meet in the gymnasium to sing songs, dance the "Hokey Pokey," and listen to a storyteller from the local public library. While the children enjoy a story time, the parents are with the reading specialist whose main goal for the evening is to educate parents on the value of reading to their children on a daily basis. Good read alouds are modeled, books shown and enjoyed, parental concerns and questions addressed, and a healthy attitude toward reading with children is nurtured.

The parents then return to the gym to sit with their child and enjoy a story from the storyteller. Then, the very best part, the parents snuggle with their children and read aloud a favorite book. We finish the evening off with a "bedtime" snack of milk and cookies.

We tried many things to boost parental involvement with mediocre results prior to initiating The Pajama Party. We have experienced great success in getting parents to participate in this annual event. It has become a tradition that is highly anticipated by all.

Title: A Sample Agenda for the Parent Meeting

The 30-minute parent meeting takes place in the school library. While the parents meet, the children remain in the gymnasium with the teachers.

Objectives:

The parents will have the opportunity to:

1. Gain understanding into the role that they play in facilitating their child's reading development.
2. Become familiar with practical strategies they can use to support reading development.

Activity:

📖 Begin by reading aloud a tradebook . You may want to consider *"Time for Bed"* by Mem Fox to model a read aloud bedtime story. Demonstrate how to read expressively, how to ask questions to get children thinking as they listen, etc.

📖 Share the importance of reading aloud. I have an overhead that reads, "The most important thing you can do for your child? READ ALOUD!"

📖 Discuss ways to find good books for reading aloud. The following resources may be helpful to parents: teachers, school and public librarians, book stores that have large children's literature sections and knowledgeable personnel, children's magazines, etc.

📖 Show books that have qualities that relate specifically to the needs of early readers. Explain how repetition and rhyme support developing readers. You may want to model using, *"Love You Forever"* by Robert Munsch.

📖 Give parents an easy-to-understand overview of the reading process. You may want to discuss the three cueing systems (visual, meaning, and structural) and give examples of how to prompt for each.

📖 Or you may prefer sharing a few practical ideas for how parents can help at home with early through fluent readers. For example: Offer suggestions for how to help children decode words. Or explain why story retellings are important and demonstrate how to prompt children to engage in a retelling.

📖 Allow time to entertain questions.

📖 Close by interactively reading a poem with the parents. *"Read To Me"* by Jane Yolen is perfect!

The parents then return to the gymnasium to enjoy a storytelling, read with their child, and have a "bedtime" snack.

Note: Make sure the parents realize that they must stay the entire time, this is not a "real" sleepover, and that parents do not need to come in their p.j.'s.

Title: A Sample Agenda for the Students

The children stay with the teachers in the gymnasium as the parents proceed to the library for the parent presentation. The entire Pajama Party lasts about one hour.

Objectives:

The children will have the opportunity to:

1. Engage in activities that promote literacy development in the motivational context of a large group.
2. Engage in interactive reading with a parent.

Activity:

- Greet the children as they arrive and pass out color-coded teddy bear nametags. Children are grouped by the color of their tag. The children sit with the teacher who is holding the teddy bear that matches their name tag color.
- Dance *"The Hokey Pokey."* Children form circles or double lines with their group members. You may want to use a tape-recorded version of the song.
- Dramatize the *"Teddy Bear, Teddy Bear Turn Around"* rhyme while chanting it aloud and reading it from an overhead projector. Select one or two children from each group to be the "shadow bears" who model the movements.
- Storytelling presentation. If you are unable to get a storyteller, you may use the following as an alternative format:
- Read aloud *Mooncake* by Frank Ashe. While one teacher reads, another points to the text that has been printed onto overhead transparencies.
- Gather the children into a large circle. One teacher leads *"I'm Going on a Bear Hunt"* as the other teachers participate and interact with the children.

The parents return to the gymnasium. They enjoy a final story from the guest storyteller. Then they read aloud to their child and together enjoy a "bedtime" snack.

Lynnette Brenner, Reading Specialist

Chapter 4: Language and Literacy Development

Title: Monthly Poetry Recital

Objectives: Children will have the opportunity to:

1. Demonstrate expressive language skills while reciting poems to a variety of audiences.
2. Increase their oral language vocabulary by learning new words from the poetry.

Materials: Copy of the poetry book *Chicken Soup with Rice* by Maurice Sendak, chart paper or overhead transparency to copy poem, materials for creating props: construction paper, scissors, crayons, markers, and craft sticks.

Activity:

📖 Select the poem from *Chicken Soup with Rice* that corresponds to the month in which this activity takes place.

📖 Copy the poem onto chart paper or onto an overhead transparency. Recite the poem for the children while encouraging them to read along. Repeat short phrases of the poem in order to help them memorize the words.

📖 Have the children practice the poem each day for one week using expression and volume appropriate for public speaking.

📖 Have the students create props to go along with the poem. For example: For the February poem from *Chicken Soup With Rice*, have the children make soup bowls, cakes, boys, and snowmen. After they have colored and cut out their props, attach craft sticks in order to use them as stick puppets.

📖 When the poem has been practiced with the puppets, have the children visit the classrooms of one grade level in your school to share the poem. Each month the children can learn a new poem from *Chicken Soup With Rice* and visit a different grade level to share their poem.

Variations:

📖 The children can create motions to the poem rather than constructing props.

📖 The children can create pictures to go along with the poem for each month of the school year. In June, you could compile a copy of each poem along with the students' pictures to create a month-by-month poetry book for the children to take home as an end of the year remembrance.

📖 Children can learn the months of the year or basic sight words from these poems.

Kimberly Knarr, Kindergarten Teacher

Title: What Am I Wearing?:
An Oral Language Development Lesson for Second Language Learners

Objectives: The children will have the opportunity to:
1. Develop oral vocabulary associated with winter clothing.
2. Engage in dialogue in a question/answer format.

Materials: *The Jacket I Wear in the Snow* by S. Neitzel, articles of clothing that are mentioned in the book to be used as props: jacket, hat, scarf, mittens, sweater, long underwear, pants, boots, zipper, etc., flannel board cut-outs of the articles of clothing, flannel board.

Activity:

📖 Have the children brainstorm to generate a list of clothing that is worn in the winter.

📖 Read aloud the story, *The Jacket I Wear in the Snow*. After reading, discuss what articles of clothing were mentioned in the story and add to the list if necessary.

📖 Distribute the articles of clothing to the students so that each has one item.

📖 Read the story a second time. This time, pause when an article of clothing is mentioned in the story. Encourage the children to hold up their item and name it when it appears in the story. For example, you will read, "This is the (sweater) I wear in the snow." The child who has the sweater will hold it up and say "sweater."

📖 Encourage the children to join in by chanting the repetitive phrases and the names of the articles of clothing as they are repeated in the story.

📖 At the conclusion of the story, re-distribute the clothing props. Ask questions such as the following:

   📖 "Who has the hat?" Expected response: "Amy has the hat."

   📖 "What color is the jacket?" Expected response: "The jacket is blue."

   📖 "What do we put on our hands to keep them warm?" Expected response: "We put mittens on our hands."

Variations:

📖 Use the flannel board and the cutouts to review the names of the articles of clothing and question/answer format. Distribute the items to the children. Give simple clues describing one of the items. Have the child who has the item put it onto the board while telling the name.

📖 Provide the children with an opportunity to work in pairs to retell the story using the book and the flannel board pieces.

Gina A. Goble, ESL Teacher Grades K-3

Title: Exploring Word Processing

Objectives: Children will have the opportunity to:
1. Become familiar with the computer keyboard.
2. Become familiar with different types of print.
3. Perform basic functions of word processing using a mouse.

Materials: Computers , printer, word processing application. (For this lesson I use "The Writing Center.")

Activity:

📖 Children should have some prior knowledge and experience with computers before engaging in this lesson (e.g., ability to use a mouse and the ability to appropriately use the keyboard).

📖 Have the students open the program, which in this case is "The Writing Center."

📖 Tell them to type their name 5 times.

📖 After they are finished, show them how to highlight one line of their work by holding down the mouse button and going back over a line of the work.

📖 Next have the students locate the word "fonts" at the top and click onto it.

📖 Show them how that each time they click onto a new word in the font list their name will look different.

📖 Once they have accomplished changing the font in one copy of their names, have them try to change each one so that no two copies of their name look the same.

📖 While they are working, go around and change all their font size to 20pt or higher so it will stand out when they are done.

📖 When all five copies of their names have been changed to different fonts, instruct the children to print out a copy.

📖 Take the copies back to the classroom. The children will enjoy putting them right on their desks for everyone to see.

Variations:

📖 If access to computers is limited, this could be done as a center activity in your classroom using one computer.

📖 Photocopy their products. Cut each name apart and put all five copies of every name into an alphabet center for sorting.

📖 Create a bulletin board with each student's picture. Place their typed names in a bag near the board and during independent work period the students can match the correct name to the correct picture.

Kathy Erickson, Special Education Teacher

Title: Visit the White House on a Virtual Tour

Objectives: Children will have the opportunity to:
1. Read the "White House for Kids" web site.
2. View the rooms that are on the public tour.
3. Answer comprehension questions and write a paragraph about the White House based upon information gleaned from the virtual tour.

Materials: Computers, pencils, pens, paper for student writing, student packet – one per student.

Activity:

📖 Show students how to type in the URL for the "White House for Kids" web site.

📖 Model how to navigate within the site using the down arrows, and the back and forward buttons.

📖 Distribute a packet to each child.

📖 Guide the students through the first page of directions and questions. Direct the students to the pictures and text on the screen to answer the questions. Discuss and respond to the information learned.

📖 Let students proceed at their own pace if it is evident that they are comfortable following the directions in the packet.

📖 After completing the packet, have the students compose an expository paragraph about the White House using the new information they learned.

Variations:

📖 The students may work in partners to complete this activity.

📖 Have students take home the web address. Perhaps they will want to share this site with their parents or siblings.

📖 Have the students make a comparison between their house and the White House. They may write a family history that includes special events that took place in their house.

📖 Provide students with a list of other web sites that offer information relating to topics of interest. Have the students compose directions and questions for a mini virtual tour.

THE WHITE HOUSE FOR KIDS ACTIVITY PACKET
http://www2.whitehouse.gov/WH/kids/html/home.html

Name: _____

Go on a tour of the White House. Follow your tour guide and answer the following questions.

1. Click on **star #1** (Location). What is the address of the White House?

2. Scroll down the page using the down arrow. Name two buildings that are pictured on the pink and green map.

3. Scroll down to the bottom of this screen. Click onto **star#2**, the blue star (History). What was the biggest house in the United States until the Civil War?

4. What is the name of the president who served the shortest term of any president?

5. Click the word **more** under the black arrow at the bottom of your screen. What president decided that Washington, D.C. would be our capital city?

6. What French man planned the city of Washington, D.C.?

7. How was the original District of Columbia (Washington, D.C.) much like a wilderness?

8. Click the word **more** at the bottom of your screen. What was the name of the architect who designed the White House?

9. Which president was the first to actually live in the White House?

10. Click on **John Adams**. (It is blue on your screen.) You will see a picture of our second president. Read the Fast Fact at the bottom of his page. What is he famous for doing?

11. Click the **Back** button at the top left corner of your screen. This will take you back to the page titled, "Constructing a Home for the President." Scroll down to the bottom. What happened to the White House while James Madison was president?

12. Dolly Madison is responsible for having saved what valuable painting of which president?

13. Click on **Dolly Madison**. It is written in blue on your screen. This means there is a **link** to another screen. What is Dolly Madison's full name?

14. Click the **Back** button at the top left-hand corner of your screen. Scroll all the way down to the bottom of your screen and click the word **more** that is under the black arrow. You should now be at a screen titled, **"The House."** How many visitors does the White House receive each day?

15. Fill in the chart. How many of each does the White House have?
    Floors___
    Rooms___
    Bathrooms___
    Windows___
    Doors___
    Chimneys___
    Elevators___
    Staircases___

16. If you go on a tour of the White House, what five rooms are you able to see?

17. Click on the word **more** at the bottom of your screen. You should now be at the screen titled, **"A Tour of the House."** Look at the picture of The Blue Room. Why is this room oval shaped?

18. Look at the picture of The Green Room. What is the most interesting thing to you about this room?

19. Look at the picture of The Red Room. What covers the walls of this room?

20. Look at the picture of The State Dining Room. How many guests can eat here?

21. What did President Theodore Roosevelt once hang above the fireplace in The State Dining Room?

22. Look at the picture of The East Room. Name at least four events for which this room is used.

23. Click the **down arrow** and scroll down to the bottom of this screen. Click the word **more** under the black arrow. Look at the picture of The Oval Office. What kinds of business does the President do here?

24. Scroll down to the bottom of this page. Click the word **more** at the bottom. You should now be back to a screen titled, "Learn More About the White House." Our tour is finished for now. List three interesting facts you learned about the White House.

Carol Bastian, Third Grade Teacher

Title: A Story Retelling of *The Foot Book* by Dr. Seuss

Objectives: Children will have the opportunity to:
1. Participate in re-enacting the story by creating a slide show.
2. Extend their understanding of opposites specific to *The Foot Book*.

Materials: A copy of the text, camera and slide film, props (socks, clown costume, water, towel, bandages, stuffed cat, stuffed guinea pig, chair, ladder, ball), poster-making materials (markers, poster board, letter stencils).

Activity:

📖 Read *The Foot Book* to the children.

📖 List the different slide pictures they are going to create by telling them that the pictures in the book will relate to the pictures they will be re-enacting.

📖 Assign children to specific pages. Have the children offer ideas and make a list of the props they will need for their picture of the re-enactment.

📖 Have the children make the posters for their page using the poster board, letter stencils, and markers. Emphasize the opposite words in the story.

📖 Photograph the children as they pose with their props and posters just like their assigned page in book.

📖 Show the slide story while having the children re-tell each page as it appears on the screen. Have the children use different tones of voice when reading the opposite word pairs.

Variations:

📖 Mount photographs reproduced from the slides into a special classroom edition of *The Foot Book*. Place it in your classroom library for the children to retell the story.

📖 Create a pack of cards that include opposite words from *The Foot Book*. Have children match the opposite words. Include blank cards for children to record their own opposite pairs. These can later be put into a class book of opposites to go along with the class rendition of *The Foot Book*.

Pat Carroll and Amy Nastus, Graduate School of Education Students

Title: A Story Retelling of
The Very Hungry Caterpillar by Eric Carle

Objectives: The children will have the opportunity to:
1. Retell the story in sequential order.
2. Identify the days of the week and the number words "one" through "five."
3. Gain understanding into the lifecycle of a butterfly.

Materials: A copy of the text, the following laminated construction paper story telling props: one apple, two pears, three plums, four strawberries, five oranges, one leaf, a variety of junk food, a cocoon, and butterfly wings. Place a strip of magnetic tape onto the back of each prop. (In most cases, these will stick to the chalkboard in your classroom. If not, try a metal stovetop cover. It works great!), days of the week and number words "one" through "five" written onto index cards.

Activity:
📖 Tell the story using the props. Invite the children to join you in the storytelling by emphasizing the story pattern and encouraging them to say the repetitive phrase.

📖 Use the props to review the sequence of the story as well as the days of the week and number of items eaten on a particular day.

📖 Guide the children in matching the days-of-the-week cards and the number word cards to the item(s) eaten. Model how to use the beginning letter of each word to decode it. Show how to check it by running their finger under each letter of the word and making sure they have a sound for each letter. Point out the repetitive "day" chunk in each of the weekday words.

📖 Place the storytelling materials along with the word cards into the classroom literacy center to allow for independent and partner retellings of the story.

Variations:

📖 Have the children look through magazines and newspaper circulars to find pictures of the items that the caterpillar ate. The children can make their own little book of the story by pasting the pictures onto pages where they write the day of the week and the number word of each item consumed.

Kyriaki Sklavounos, First Grade Teacher

Title: Letter Writing to Corduroy the Bear

Objectives: The children will have the opportunity to:
1. Learn about the parts of an informal letter
2. Apply that knowledge by writing a letter to Corduroy

Materials: A copy of the books *Corduroy* and *A Pocket for Corduroy* by Don Freeman, chart paper to record students' responses, large mailbox , "Letterman," (see diagram), letter from Corduroy written on large chart paper, paper, envelopes, and pencils for letter writing, stuffed Corduroy bear.

Activity:

📖 Over a period of two days, read aloud the Corduroy books. Model some things you would like to ask Corduroy or say to him if you had the chance. Have the children offer the same while you record their statements and questions onto chart paper.

📖 After school on the second day, Corduroy "visits" your classroom and leaves a big mailbox, a stuffed Corduroy, and a letter saying, "Dear Boys and Girls, I am so happy that you are reading stories about me. Since we can't talk in person, you can write a letter to me and I'll write back! Love, Corduroy."

📖 Explain to the children that they first must learn how to write a letter in order to correspond with Corduroy. Introduce "Letterman" who will "save the day" by showing them how it's done. "Letterman" displays the three parts of a letter- the heading, the body, and the closing.

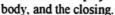

- Explain and model each part by writing a sample letter to Corduroy. Refer to the comments and questions generated on the two previous days.
- Give students the opportunity to write to Corduroy by following the model.
- "Mail" the letters and enjoy the fun when the children get a response from Corduroy. (Older students love reading and answering the letters that the children write to Corduroy. It's an authentic letter writing activity for them, too.)

Variations:

- The children may enjoy listening to *The Jolly Postman* by Janet and Allan Ahlberg.
- Find a class of older students to be in-school pen pals with your students. Encourage letter writing on a regular basis.
- Introduce the children to e-mail letter writing.

Angela Feola, Second Grade Teacher

Chapter 7: Developing Concepts About Books and Comprehension of Texts

Title: Character Connections

Objectives: The children will have the opportunity to:
1. Provide literal recall of a character and his or her actions in a book.
2. Make inferential judgments about a character's behaviors.
3. Make personal connections with a character.

Materials: 2 ½ sheets of 8 1/2" by 11' paper per child, supplies for drawing: markers, crayons, pencils.

Activity:

- Prepare a master copy of the pages for the character activity as follows:
- Divide each sheet in half. You should have five rectangles
- On first half-sheet, make a cover titled "My Book About____" Add spaces for the book title, author and illustrator's names, and child's name.
- On the second half sheet, write, "What _____ looks like."

📖 On the third half sheet, write, "What ____ does."

📖 On the fourth write, "_____ would like to…"

📖 On the fifth write, "_____ is like me because…"

📖 Photocopy enough copies for each child and then cut and staple the books in order.

📖 Instruct the children to select one character from a shared story. Have them add the character's name to the front cover, along with the other information requested.

📖 Model creating a character book by walking through each page. Demonstrate how to look through text to determine what the character looks like and does (pages 2 and 3), deciding what the character might do if he or she were real (page 4), and how the character is like them (page 5).

📖 Have the students create their character book by using pictures, print or a combination thereof.

📖 Allow time for a whole class or small group sharing of the character books.

Variations:

📖 The students may write paragraphs using the information from their books to describe their character. These can be presented as dramatic narratives where the children dress like the character and orally present their paragraph.

📖 The same format can be applied to reading expository texts. Children may create a book that demonstrates their comprehension and degree of understanding about factual material.

📖 Children may create books that depict the sequence of events in a story in order to help them internalize story structure.

Margaret G Niemiec, Reading Specialist

Title: An Introduction to Graphic Organizers

Objectives: The children will have the opportunity to:

1. Gain an understanding about the purpose and meaning of a Venn diagram.
2. Use a Venn diagram to organize information.

Materials: Copy of the book Little *Blue and Little Yellow* by Leo Lionni, large chart of a blank Venn diagram, a yellow, blue, and green marker, an apple and an orange, photocopies of a Venn diagram for student use.

Activity:

📖 Read the book *Little Blue and Little Yellow* to the students.

📖 After reading the story, display the large Venn diagram. Provide the children with an opportunity to comment on how the Venn diagram reminds them of the characters in the story.

📖 Have the children retell the story. Prompt them as needed. During the retelling, use the markers to color in the circles of the diagram to look like the book characters "hugging" one another as they do in the story. Discuss how the center of the diagram is what they have in common.

📖 Use this as a springboard to compare and contrast the apple and the orange. As the children suggest similarities and differences between the two fruits, model how and where to record them on the diagram.

📖 Distribute the student copies of the Venn diagram. Have the children work in pairs to compare and contrast a pear and a lime.

Variations:

📖 Venn diagrams can be used to teach primary and secondary colors. Make watercolors and blank Venn diagrams available in the art center and have the children experiment with mixing colors.

Danielle D. Lynch, Kindergarten Teacher

Chapter 8: Word Study Skills: Phonemic Awareness and Phonics

Title: Integrating Phonics Instruction into the Morning Message

Objectives: Children will have the opportunity to:

1. Learn how knowledge of word families facilitates decoding of words.
2. Use context clues as a means of decoding unknown words.

Materials: Chart paper, markers, sticky notes.

Activity:

☐ Compose a morning message on scrap paper that uses words from the "at" word family. Circle the words that belong to the "at" family and then cross out the initial consonant. For example: *Today, we will have John's cat visit our classroom. The last time Sylvester was here, he sat on the rug. We will sit on our mats while John shows his cat. This will be fun!*

☐ Re-write the message onto chart paper omitting the initial consonant of all the "at" family words. Example: *Today we will have John's _at visit our classroom. The last time Sylvester was here, he _at on the rug. We will sit on our _ats while John shows us his _at. This will be fun!*

☐ Show the Morning Message to the students, explaining that letters are missing. Read the message aloud encouraging the children to read along. Everyone claps when they come across a missing letter.

☐ To begin the process for problem solving the unknown words, ask the children to tell you what information they DO know after reading the first sentence of the message. Students may, for example, say, "Something is visiting." Or, "It's something that belongs to John."

☐ Based upon the known information, generate a list of possible letters that would make sense in the missing space. As students respond, write their guesses onto a sticky note and place it in the blank in order to provide a visual link for problem solving.

☐ Ask students what the best choice would be. Write the correct letter onto the chart. Have the students read the sentence to check if it makes sense and sounds right. Repeat these steps with the reminder of the morning message.

☐ When all the blanks are filled with the correct letters, read the complete message. You may have the class read chorally or may select a few students to read.

Variations:

☐ As children become more adept at applying word analysis skills, you may focus on more than one word family within a morning message. You may also misspell words and eliminate punctuation and ask the children to identify the errors.

Jeanne Velechko, Third Grade Teacher

Title: Understanding Homophones

Objectives: Children will have the opportunity to:
1. Identify homophones.
2. Demonstrate understanding of when each word in a pair of homophones should be used.

Materials: Index cards-one per student for every homophone pair presented in the lesson, markers, sentence strips with pre-written sentences that contain each word of a homophone pair.

Activity:

📖 Create a list of easily confused homophones. The list should include the homophones your students spell incorrectly when writing. Some possibilities include:

its	it's	
to	too	two
there	their	they're

📖 Introduce the term "homophone" by explaining that at times we hear words that sound the same, but are spelled differently. Emphasize the need to use the correct spelling since it affects the meaning of a sentence.

📖 Provide a model by showing and reading aloud two sentence strips that each contains one word of a pair of homophones. For example, Strip 1 will read, "I have a bee buzzing around me!" Strip 2 will read, "Will you be at my party?"

📖 Have the students identify the pair of homophones. Discuss spelling and meaning differences between the homophones.

📖 Have the students write the homophones (*be* and *bee*) onto an index card, one word on each side of the card.

📖 Continue by reading another sentence strip that contains one word of the pair. This time, do not allow the students to see the sentence.

📖 Instruct the students to hold up their index card so that it indicates the form of the homophone they expect to see in the sentence. Show the sentence strip and discuss the correct answer.

📖 Repeat this process using several sentences.

Variations:

📖 When teaching sight word vocabulary, children can use scrap paper cut to the size of index cards to write sight words. Say the word, have the students write it onto their paper, and hold it up for a quick class check.

Jeanne Velechko, Third Grade Teacher

Title: Script a Play

Objectives: Children will have the opportunity to:
1. Develop their writing abilities while working cooperatively.
2. Practice writing dialog that incorporates expressive language and correct punctuation associated with writing speech.

Materials: A variety of dress-up clothes and props (purses, briefcases, etc.), writing paper and pencils.

Activity:

📖 Send children in small groups to the area of the room where the dress-up clothes and props are located. Allow the children time to explore the items in order to decide which props they would like to use and clothing they would like to wear as a costume. The children then decide which character they would like to play.

📖 Together the children compose a story that includes the character each created. Each child writes the story so that each one has his or her own copy of the script.

📖 Once the play is written, the children show it to the teacher. Suggestions may be made for editing and revising.

📖 The children then dress in their costumes to rehearse and dramatize the play. On occasion, plays may be performed for the class or for another appreciative audience.

Variations:

📖 Costumes, puppets, or masks that relate to storybook characters may be placed in the dress-up area along with corresponding pieces of literature. The children may write plays based upon these familiar characters and stories.

Fran Regis, First Grade Teacher

Title: Journal Starters

Objectives: Children will have the opportunity to:
1. Develop a tool that is self-selected and easily accessible for prompting journal writing

Materials: Pocket folders- one per student, scissors, magazines, newspapers, old calendars, other sources of pictures, markers.

Activity:

📖 Give the students each a folder asking them to label it with their names and decorate it as desired using the markers.

📖 Explain to the students that they will be writing in their journals on a daily basis. There may be days when they have difficulty thinking of a topic on which to write. Therefore, they are going to create a folder of pictures they can use whenever they need an idea to spark their writing.

📖 Provide students with the various magazines and newspapers from which to select and cut out pictures that interest them. Pictures are then placed in the folders.

📖 Encourage the children to bring in photographs or pictures from home to add to their folder at any point in the school year.

Variations:

📖 The children's picture collections may also be used to spark story writing or used as illustrations for stories children have written.

Jennifer Haik, Second Grade Teacher

Chapter 10: Organizing and Managing the School Learning Environment for Literacy Development

Title: Finding a "Just Right" Book for Independent Reading

Objectives: The children will have the opportunity to:
1. Gain understanding into different levels of text and how that affects their reading.
2. Practice identifying books that are within their independent reading level.

Materials: A variety of leveled books that represent a wide span of levels, pan balance, objects to be weighed, photocopies of blank pan balances for student use.

Activity:

This portion of the lesson is carried out in a whole class context:

📖 In pairs, have the students share with each other things that they find very easy to do and activities that they find very challenging. Model by sharing something that's easy for you and something that you find very hard to carry out.

📖 After a few minutes of sharing, reconvene as a whole group and discuss the topic. Highlight the fact that things that are easy for one may not be easy for another and vice versa.

📖 Show the pan balance. Explain how the pan balance shows the heaviness of an object. Describe how activities that are too hard leave you feeling "weighted down," like the pan balance with heavy weight. Activities that are too easy represent the pan balance that is suspended in the air. "There's nothing to it." Then display the pan balance with equivalent weights. Explain how it is perfectly balanced or "just right."

📖 Have the children return to their pairs and work together to complete the diagrams of the pan balances by writing their hard activities on the low pan, their easy activities on the high pan and their "just right" activities in the middle.

The following portion of the lesson takes place in small groups:

📖 Review the concept of the pan balance as it relates to things people do. Explain that it also relates to books. Show samples of texts that are too hard. Discuss their qualities (too many words, no pictures, too many words that need decoding, etc.) Place them on the pan balance so the pan lowers dramatically.

📖 Do the same with books that are too easy. Place fewer of them in the pan balance so they are significantly lighter. Remove the books from the balance.

📖 Then discuss "just right" books by describing the specific characteristics for which the children should be looking. Place them on the scale so that both sides are equivalent in weight.

📖 Have each child apply the information by looking for a "just right" book. Monitor their process.

Note: A poster depicting a balanced scale and the words "Just Right" may serve as a reminder to the students.

Danielle D. Lynch, Kindergarten Teacher

Title: A Small Group Guided Reading Lesson for Early Readers: A Sample of Explicit Instruction for Kindergarten –Second Grade

Objectives: The children will have the opportunity to:
1. Engage in a small group lesson crafted to their individual needs as developing readers.
2. Develop the strategies necessary for independent reading.

Materials: One copy per student of a text selected for its inherent qualities that will allow for skill and strategy instruction. (Note: The text must be in the instructional reading level of the children. That means the children should be able to read 90-94% of the text accurately and with good comprehension prior to the lesson.) Additional useful materials: white boards and markers for teacher and student use, magnetic letters, chart paper on a stand.

A Guided Reading Lesson Format:

The text used in this sample lesson is *Tricking Tracy* published by Rigby. In this story, a girl named Tracy plays tricks on others by pretending to be in trouble. Shortly, those around her realize that she is not in need of assistance when she asks. One day, her trick backfires and she really does need help. This time no one comes to her aid.

📖 **Introduction to the Text:** Generate a <u>brief</u> conversation that stimulates the children's background knowledge related to the text.

📖 " Have you played a trick on anyone? Did the person you tricked think it was funny? Did you ever have someone play a trick on you that you didn't like?"

📖 **Book Walk or Picture Walk:** Guide the children through the text by discussing the text illustrations. You may walk through the entire text or choose only certain pages to discuss. Bring forward any concepts related to comprehending the text that you think might be new or challenging for the children in the group. The book walk should be tailored to the needs of the children.

📖 In *Tricking Tracy*, you may discuss the worried looks on the character's faces when they thought that Tracy was in trouble. Have the children hypothesize how they think the characters felt when they learned she was only tricking.

📖 Word work may be integrated into the book walk. You may ask the children to locate certain words or apply problem-solving strategies together before having the children read the book independently.

📖 In this text, some children have difficulty with the words "only" and "always." Discussing the strategy of looking for known "chunks" in an unknown word and applying it to decoding these two words may be useful.

📖 **Children Read the Text Independently and Silently:** Set a purpose for reading and instruct the children to begin. While they read, circulate among the group members asking them to quietly read aloud when you crouch next to them. If the children are not yet ready to read silently, instruct them to read very quietly. Make sure the children understand that they are not to read chorally. Circulate among the group and listen-in on individual readers.

📖 **Individual Strategy Instruction:** As you listen to individual children read, prompt their thinking toward developing reading strategies. Respond to their miscues in such a way that they learn to synthesize all the of information sources readers use. The following examples offer suggestions of such prompts:

- When children miscue by making a meaningless substitution, you may say, "Does that makes sense? Look at the picture. Would that be right? Think about what you read so far. Would that belong in this story?"

- When children miscue by not monitoring their language use, you can ask, "Does that sound right? Do we talk like that? Listen to what you read (you repeat). What doesn't sound right about it?"

- When children fail to use the letters in a word as an information source, you can ask, "Does that look right? Point and check if you have a sound for every letter? Is there a little word in the big word that you know?"

- Be sure to praise self-correction, the use of self-monitoring strategies, expressive reading, and fluency.

- If the children are reading short texts, you may ask them to read it again. You may also instruct them to read with a partner. This will give you additional time to do individual instruction.

- **Group Instruction:** Based upon your assessment and observation of the children as they read the text, conduct a mini-lesson based on their needs. This may include compound words, suffixes, prefixes, punctuation, rhyming words, fluency, comprehension skills such as inferencing, etc.

- **Follow-Up:** Not every book used in a guided reading lesson is followed by an activity. Some may lend themselves to artistic or dramatic connections that enhance the story meaning. Most often, follow-up simply consists of taking the book home to re-read it, placing it in a book basket for independent reading, or being assigned new pages to read which will be discussed the next time the group meets.

Elizabeth Asbury, Rutgers University

NOTES

NOTES

NOTES

NOTES

NOTES

NOTES

NOTES

NOTES

NOTES

NOTES

NOTES

NOTES

NOTES

NOTES